Genitology
Reading the Genitals

By:
Dr. Seymore Klitz
and
Dr. Ima Peeper

Illustrations by La Tour

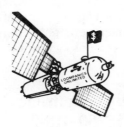

Loompanics Unlimited
Port Townsend, Washington

Genitology

Reading the Genitals

By:

Dr. Seymore Klitz
and
Dr. Ima Peeper

Illustrations by La Tour

Published by:

Loompanics Unlimited
PO Box 1197
Port Townsend, WA 98368

© 1989 by Loompanics Unlimited
ISBN 1-55950-018-2

First published in 1983 by Gen Publications
Printed in the U.S.A.

Dedication

This book is dedicated to
each and everyone of you with genitals,
for without you
this book could not have been written.

Note From the Publisher

When this manuscript first arrived on our desk we were shocked to say the least. But after recovering we began to see that this really is quite a piece of work, and very funny at that. We have published it in our final belief that this area needs more humorous exposure and is something that people should face squarely. Hopefully this book will help.

The manuscript has been published as received with only the most minor editorial changes, preserving the satirical tone of the original. We can only apologize in advance if anybody feels offended. All references to known personages are purely in the spirit of the satirical nature of the work.

The authors have asked that they remain anonymous to protect their reputations in other fields.

Prologue

In recent years a tremendous resurgence of interest has arisen in the genitals. With this arousal has come a reformulation of the ancient principles into the modern science of Genitology. It is based on ageless wisdom, nevertheless it has taken the thrust of modern research to truly bring together these ancient principles in a form that can be embraced by modern man.

In fact research has grown at such a voracious rate that voluminous piles of unevaluated material began to clog my office and overflow into the hall. A solution had to be found, and found it was. Drs. Klitz and Peeper have done such a marvelous job of condensing and collating the information into the small volume you now hold in your hands, that I have had all that paperwork dumped in the trash. I can now get into my office without snowshoes.

Do not be fooled. This is the cream of research. What you have here is a compact manual of intensely useful material that will, in a few short hours, start you on the road to successfully reading genitals. Be prepared to amaze your friends and confound your enemies with the information you find here.

I personally highly recommend this book for anyone considering getting into the area of the genitals.

Sincerely,

Dr. Izzard T. Snooglehorne
Dean of the School of Genitological Anthropology
University of Twatdiddle
Whatapecka, FL
June, 1983

Table of Contents

History
of
Genitology

History of Genitology

It is obvious that from the earliest of times people have had an interest in the genitals. This interest stems from a basic subconscious understanding that the shape and size of a person's genitals reflects the individual's personality characteristics. This intuitive understanding was the driving force behind the creation of various systems and activities which, over the centuries, culminated in the science we now know as Genitology.

For millenia men, women and children have been fascinated by the mysterious genitals. It would be safe to say that in one form or another everyone has made an informal study of Genitology, be it through Playboy magazines or playing doctor at age 5. Who has not experienced that strong curiosity to know what was under the clothes we are made to wear so early in life? Peepholes, peepshows, bottomless nightclubs, Playboys, and Playgirls, all attest to this curiosity. What man has not dropped a pencil in class at one time or another hoping for a quick beaver shot? But beyond the casual approach, there have been various individuals in certain societies who made this a life long dedicated study— complete with carefully kept records of their observations.

Much of the information we are about to cover was well known in earlier civilizations only to be lost with the coming of more repressive societies closer to the present day. This is not to say that research ever ceased entirely. It is only that the individuals who continued to carry the torch for Genitology were forced undercovers, so to speak, and their findings carefully hidden until these facts could once again seek the light of day. And indeed that day has come with the publication of this book.

Neanderthal Man

The first known Genitological studies are to be found on the walls of ancient caves in France. (Fig.1) Studies have shown that these drawings trace all the way back to the Neanderthal man, some 10,000 years ago. Certainly these were the first graffiti. The

Fig.1 Ancient ubangers depicted in primitive drawings found in the Lascoux caves in France

drawings depict stick figure men with erect penises proudly walking the earth, showing off their member for all to see. Undoubtedly these were illustrations of Nightsticks (see the Joystick section), and even in that far time it was something to brag about.

China

Cave drawings have also been found in China. Dated circa 3000 B.C. these drawings were less primitive and showed the ancient whangers in more detail as well as the first known depiction of the vagina. In one classic drawing five male figures are lined up with genitals well exposed. Our own careful study has shown that four of the known eight male types are represented. In this particular scene there is also a woman standing to one side observing the men. The next drawing shows her having intercourse with one of them. It is fascinating to realize that she has chosen the male with Le Long Carabine, and that her reading shows her to be a Venus Man Trap, a perfect match according to modern Genitological standards!

Also found in these caves were strangely carved jade rings (Fig.2). These soon became part of the "Rosetta Stone" of Genitology. When first found the rings were a mystery to archeologists as they were obviously too large for fingers. It was only a tragic accident that brought their true use to light

One night a kinky member of the expedition slipped a ring on his whanger before beating off. Unfortunately he picked one of the smaller rings, and before another member of the expedition could help him be had done himself considerable damage. This was a terrible tragedy for a single man, but a giant leap forward for mankind. The hypothesis was suggested that these rings had something to do with the penis. (Incidentally the debilitated member was a Dented Dick, of which more later.)

Further excavation proved this hypothesis as more rings were found with descriptive inscriptions on the inside. These inscriptions translated to small, large, long and short, or our

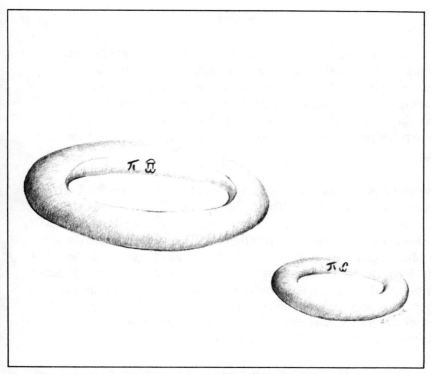

*Fig.2 Jade penis rings found in the Hung-Far-Low
anthropological excavations. Note inscriptions:
Top left—the Cock, Bottom right—the Bamboo Shoot.*

modern equivalent of Pinky, Nightstick, Long Carabine, and Dork.
The piece de resistance came when deep in one excavation a
stone tablet was found depicting the use of the rings. The ring was
placed at the base of the root, and upon erection the restriction of
blood flow out of the penis allowed it to remain erect for hours.
The mystery was solved.

There has been much debate in Genitological circles whether the
"Penetta Stone", as it has come to be called, predates the Kama
Sutra, or if it is merely a translation of the work brought to China.
It is an important scholastic question as it seeks to identify our
true Genitological forbearers.

India

Next our historical journey takes us to India. We have already mentioned the Kama Sutra, undoubtedly the most famous Genitological book known. This book was the culmination of years of arduous Indian research and experimentation in sexuality. Much of this research was documented in the well known friezes found on ancient temples and buildings of that era (Fig.3).

The Indians had an elaborated system of classification for both penile and vaginal types. The Indian system found three of each type. Male were classified as Hare (small), Bull (medium), and Stallion (large); female as Gazelle (small), Mare (medium), and Elephant (large). Modern methods have found eight male and five female types, as well as many variations on each. Further the Sutra investigated the potential matchups between male and female types. This was truly an advanced work for so ancient a people, Modern Genitologists are still awed at the range of nuance appreciated by the Indian researchers.

It is not generally realized in the West what wealth of material still remains to be translated from the East. Indian scholars estimate that there are at least 125,000 Indian works needing translation. A cursory study by a Genitological researcher turned up an ancient Indian practice of genital reading at birth. According to this researcher the reading was as important as the astrological chart.

In his article, "Indian Genitological Philosophy—The Rise and Fall of the Ancient Whanger", the researcher details what he found. As a body grows, the genitals change. The Indians felt that knowledge of the original state of the genitals was vital to correct interpretation of later readings. They would plot these changes throughout life, thereby spotting trends that were used in divination.

We have included this bit of information to show how far the Indians had advanced in this science, in some instances even

Fig. 3 An Indian frieze found in the Uttar Pradesh province depicting penile and vaginal types. From L to R: The Spike, The Butterfly, The Mouth, The Cock, The Bamboo Shoot.

surpassing modern techniques. It is also a plea for more people to enter research in this vital area, as truly there is much more in depth exploration to be done.

Egypt

Next we consider the Genitological mysteries of Egypt. This culture included many secret societies, the priesthood being the most secret of them all. Modern scholars have interpreted much of the ancient materials—palmistry, astrology, sun worship— but one does not often hear of the undecipherable parchments and friezes which have been found. Possibly it was the historians' Puritanical background that blinded them to the meaning of Genitological artifacts, and caused them to keep the scrolls from the public eye. Any untrained person could easily see the symbology in the ancient hieroglyphics (Fig.4). The stone tablet depicted in the illustration is typical of artifacts unearthed but uninterpreted. This stone was found as a paperweight on a noted Egyptologist's desk. It was the source of much humor in the office, but the fact that it was a true relic and required serious study was never considered.

The ancient records tell a fascinating story of the priesthood. Ostensibly built up around astrology and palmistry, the priests spent most of their time practicing Genitology. The Egyptians were a symbol oriented society, and their use of the snake on the headdress was no accident. The snake symbolized the penis. And the ankh, Egyptian symbol for life, was a marrying of a symbolic penis and vagina.

The highest order of the priesthood specialized in genital reading. Their earliest function was classification of the genitalia prior to marriage. In Egyptian society premarital sex was forbidden. In order to avoid unpleasant surprises on the wedding night the parents would have the couple checked for compatibility before the marriage was arranged. A male priest would check the bride and a female the groom.

Fig. 4 Egyptian hieroglyphics discussing the compatibility of penile and vaginal types.

Later, this priesthood sought to increase its powers and began to promote readings for other purposes, such as examinations to determine fitness for political or military office. This led to the priesthood's eventual downfall.

For, as the priest's power grew, so did their enemies. A bad reading could, and did, end many a career. Bribery and corruption sprang up. As these spread, the credibility of the priesthood was destroyed. At a very crucial point those malaigned by the corrupt priests took control and managed to remove mention of the priests and their works from many important records of Egyptian history.

This was extremely unfortunate, as correct reading of the genitals can presage a man's abilities. One might even speculate that if the priesthood had remained pure Egypt may have continued as a major power in the world until today.

As a curious note the split between the Egyptians and the Jews actually had its inception in a Genitological controversy. The Jews persisted in circumcising their new born sons in defiance of the priesthood's edict that this practice be abandoned. The priests felt it interfered with their delicate readings. As part of their religion the Jews refused, and there the 2500 year old schism began. (Incidentally, modern researchers find the effect of the foreskin in the reading to be negligible.)

Only careful research and a willingness to see what is there, be it unconventional or not, has led to the discovery of this information. We expect much more information of this nature to surface, as Genitology becomes an accepted and respected science in the modern world.

Greece

The seed of Genitology was exported to Greece across the Mediterranean. The charts and understandings, so carefully developed in the secret back rooms of the Egyptian temples, were carried into the caves of the Delphic Oracle. Deep within Mt.

Olympus, patrons seeking a prophecy were often hypnotized or put to sleep by the famous vapors emanating from volcanic crevices. While in reverie the subjects robes were removed and a complete genital reading was done to supply the key information needed for the divination. This is not well known as the Oracle carefully shrouded the techniques in mystery to preserve their favored position as the preeminent fortune tellers of Greece. Although the Grecians used Genitological information, as far as we know they added nothing new to the science.

Rome

The Romans were great ones for copying the Greeks. They assimilated many of the Grecian arts and sciences, including Genitology. But Genitology never reached out into the masses of Roman society. It was an arcane study practiced and used by the Patricians, and hidden from the people. It is not well known, but the later Roman orgies were actually a serruptitious use of Genitological knowledge for political gain.

Genitological information had remained arcane, and the few who possessed this knowledge used it in the service of well placed Roman politicans for high fees. Orgies were set up to provide a means to view the genitals of enemies and thereby get readings covertly. The weaknesses discovered were used to undermine the careers of the hapless participants. This devious use of the science threw it into disrepute, much as in Egypt, and with the coming of the Christians it went underground once again.

The Dark Ages

The light of Genitology almost flickered out as the Roman Empire died and Europe slipped into the Dark Ages. And dark they were as the coming of the Christian religion and its heavy suppression of sexuality (and Genitology!) brought in the Dark Ages with a vengeance. Seeking new knowledge was a forbidden pursuit, and many of the more inquisitive in the society had to resort to secret cults to continue their quest for knowledge.

Strangely the cult that did the most to save the ancient wisdom of Genitology were the Satanists. Anything that was known to have come from the barbaric world was branded heretical. Only those courageous men who worshipped the ideals which were opposed by the Church had the balls to preserve writings, which if discovered, would cost them their lives.

For a period of 500 or more years, up to the Renaissance, Genitology was kept alive by the Satanists in their secret rites and writings. As far as we can deduce a reading of the genitals was a highly symbolic and especially favored part of the Black Mass. New initiates were required to bare their genitals on the altar, whereupon a reading was done to verify the initiates suitability for the sect. A Satanical document which recently came to light contains notes indicating that one initiate was rejected for having the modern day equivalent of the Pinky!

The Renaissance

The weak flicker of Genitology having persisted through the Dark Ages exploded into a raging bush fire in the Renaissance. Romantic love sprang onto the scene.

Before that time marriage and procreation were a practical matter. Marriages were commonly arranged to gain the maximum benefit for the family. The ideal that men and women should marry for "love" was unknown. Coincident with the birth of the Renaissance genitals were once more thrust into view. Poems and songs about love and lust became the fashion. The poets became adept at couching crude allusions to the ladies' nether parts in the most idyllic language. There was a definite perception that all pussies were not alike, and this perception was artfully crafted into the literary works of the day.

As the fire burned to its height in Europe and expecially in France, new fashions appeared. Codpieces became the rage. These pouches held the genitals in prominent display before the public, advertising the wearers make and model, so to speak. The

20

pouches became gaudy in some circles, even sporting wild red tassles to ostentatiously tantalize the viewer with flashy movement (Fig.5).

The women were not to be left out. They wore dresses with plunging necklines displaying their large bosoms and accentuating the cleavage. And, although this may be controversial, the bustle was actually introduced so that the lady could give a quick flash of her "sign" by simply leaning forward and flicking up the back of her dress. The bustle held the dress away from the buns to accomodate easy viewing.

Under these circumstances stultification of the Dark Ages blew away and Genitologists (although they knew not the name) came out of the wood work in droves. Codpieces were designed for a fast drop and dresses for a fast lift. Obviously there was much examination and exploration going on at this time. And no place was there more action than in the courts, especially the courts of France. The ladies constantly gossiped about the men's sizes and shapes while the men would laugh uproariously as they described some maid's Prissy Pussy. Although much of this was innocent fun, and far from being any sort of true Genitological study, it did open the door and let in the breath of fresh air needed to bring the ancient wisdom once again to light, and guarantee its preservation.

Puritanism

As the Renaissance waned the Church once more suppressed the merriment of the populace and we entered the Puritanical age. This reduced Genitology practice to mere smoldering embers, and then to ashes. It seems that for a period of some 200 years the light faded from the scene. Ancient volumes once more found their way into hidden libraries and private collections. There they were carefully preserved by the truly enlightened, against the ravages of the ignorant.

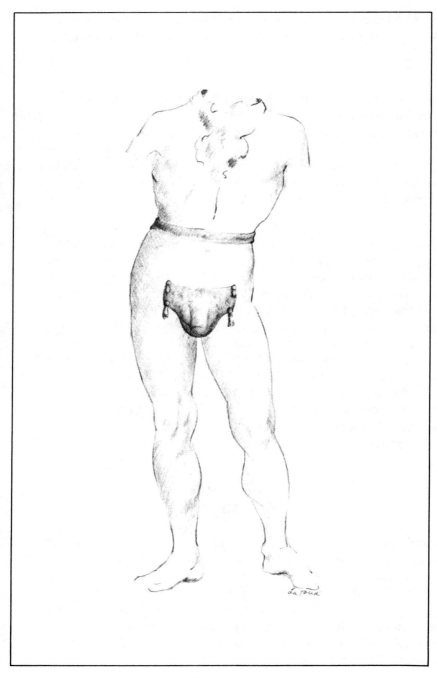

Fig.5 Red tassled codpiece from the Renaissance Period.

Modern Times

It was a chance discovery in France, in 1947, which actually set the stage for modern Genitology. A young student happened upon an ancient volume in the attic of a venerable old societe dame. His curiosity was aroused by the magnificent pictures of Nightsticks and Butterflys captioned in Old French and Latin. They roused his curiosity to the point that he was willing to undertake the momumental task of translating the ancient tongues into the modern languages. The result of his work was a small paperbound volume called "Genitology et les Parties Genitales de l'Anciens".

This circulated widely from hand to hand, as the student had included drawing from the old text. Although it created a major furor and a famous scandal, it did awaken the world once again to Genitology. As this venerable science approached the present day, undercover movements kept the flame alive. Genitology now comes to full flower, blooming in the light of day and casting its full brilliance on gentitals everywhere.

This work is a compilation of all earlier materials and new research data. It accurately aligns all data, both ancient and modern, making it available with techniques for application.

We proudly bring forth this ancient wisdom from the exclusive view of scholars, and present it to modern man. For we feel it is vital in this modern world for all to have a firm grasp of Genitological fundamentals on the one hand, and a firm grasp of the genitals with the other. We think you will agree.

The Joystick

The Joystick

Now we begin our study of the basic characteristics of the fascinating Joystick, also known as the penis. This throbbing member, the center of so much attention and interest, is about to have its secrets revealed. For indeed the Joystick is connected to the man and therefore reflects his nature.

We will be scrutinizing this wonderous instrument from many angles, just as you will be while becoming proficient in the study of Genitology. We use all parts of the whanger and their interrelationships in our attempt to get as complete an understanding as possible. Here we take up each separate aspect of the Joystick. Later we discuss how the various aspects combine to produce the different types and classifications.

The Shaft

The shaft, or root, signifies the basic character of the man. Is it short or long, thick or thin? Basically a thick shaft signifies good strong genetic stock. The body tends to be healthy. Only his tendency towards gross excesses in eating and drinking (especially beer) will eventually drag it down. The man also tends to be coarser. You are unlikely to find him at the ballet, unless he has been dragged there unwillingly by an aspiring woman. Tradesmen commonly have the "thick stick" (as it is known to those in this science). Just as their bodies seem rather insensitive to the poundings of the environment, so the owners of the thick stick are also insensitive to other people. Many of these people have good hearts, and it is this feature which so often pulls them through. But when you get a bad apple he can be really bad. Al Capone is an excellent example of the thick stick gone bad.

The thin shaft is more ephemeral. Artists and other more cerebral types fall into this category. Their bodies are not as robust. You will find them becoming vegetarians, or hanging out at the health spas. They have much more concern for the body's health because

26

they are more sensitive to its protests when they abuse it. Their problems in life stem more from not forging ahead towards what they want because of their concern and sensitivity for other people.

If the shaft is long it points toward a flexible nature. The person will tend to "go with the flow" more. For example, this is even true of the Nightstick (the long thick shafted pecker). His thick shaft shows his domineering nature. But the length reflects his basic motivation to have a good time. Witness the fraternity jock.

Conversely the short shaft is more rigid. He also doesn't have as much fun. He will push through where others will quit. This is especially true of short thick shafted fellows.

The Head

The head size denotes passion or lack of it. Large head, large passion; small head, small passion. It is basically a measure of emotion in the larger sphere. The Toad Stool for instance with his short thin shaft, but large head has quite a problem. He is basically the intellectual professorial type, but his large head makes for a reservoir of passion that often finds its outlet with young college girls.

Heads come in a variety of shapes. Pointed, flared, and flat are the basic shapes from which all heads are made.

The flared head is the style most often seen. The edge of the head flares to some degree away from the shaft. If this aspect is not pronounced it has no appreciable effect on the personality. It is the head of most men.

The pointed head is considerably rarer, and denotes a rather sly type of fellow. He's smooth and slick, and it is difficult to tell when he is telling the truth. In fact in the extreme stages of pointedness he becomes the compulsive liar. Ladies, if you suddenly find yourself faced with a pointed head, know you are in a peculiar situation. If all you want is his root, then go ahead, because it is all you are going to get.

The flat head is the rarest type. This is the head of nerds and geniuses. These fellows are an odd breed, and to date no hard and fast rules have been found to accurately predict the effect of the flat head. Suffice to say that they all exhibit some odd or unusual characteristic.

You, as the student, must realize that in all of Genitology the observations about the various types are just tendencies. When doing a reading a tremendous number of aspects are taken into consideration. Each aspect is a tendency. The art and skill of the Genitologist is to properly blend these aspects into a true whole. None of these observations are cast in stone. The interpretation of each aspect has to fit into the whole picture. If the interpretation of an aspect clashes with other aspects in the case, then the interpretation must be modified to create a unified whole.

Next we explore in depth the two basic modifiers which color all readings: the Hang (flaccid state) and the Erection. When doing a reading these considerations must be applied to all types.

How's It Hanging?

This usually unnoticed but vital fact forms an important part of any man's reading. And what is this fact? It is the predominent direction that a man's whanger hangs when a man's whanger is hanging in its unerected state. As already mentioned this is usually unnoticed, so take a moment to observe the penis. It is best observed after a shower, well dried, and shaken out (see section on "How To Do A Correct Reading"). Being stuffed into a pair of pants all day can give a false reading, so this is important.

Next, for the purposes of classification, left is defined as on the left hand side of the body from the viewpoint of the pecker's ower. With this in mind notice the prominent direction that the penis tends to seek. In the majority of men the penis will tend to the left.

You can actually verify this for yourself. The next time you are walking down the street notice which side the bulge is on. You will find that at least 80% of the men bulge on the left. Obviously it can also hang right or, on rare occasions point straight forward. The tip may also incline in a more upward direction, or turn noticibly downward. Each of these orientations has meaning and we will discuss each in turn.

Hang Left

As already mentioned this is the most common orientation. This man is more likely to go along with the current trends in society, generally following the norm, and not tending to be too radical in his thinking or behavior. This has to be throughly understood, because it does not mean the man will not be a radical. If he finds himself in a radical society, then he is likely to take on those attributes. For example if he was white and living in America in the 1950's he tended to wear a crew cut, had a house in the surburbs, and two kids. But if he lived in Berkeley in the '60's he wore his hair long and smoked marijuana. It is that he takes on the general characteristics of the society around him.

Notice that none of this is cast in stone. These aspects of the reading are very general and only delineate tendencies. In the reading they are the coloration through which one views the other aspects.

Hang Right

This man is the radical in the sense that he may or may not go along with the current norms. He may be the scientist boldly espousing now theories in the face of the old, or the leader of a communal group experimenting with new styles of living. Or if the current norms suit his personality be can champion them just as well. He is an individualist.

Hang Straight

This is an exceedingly rare individual. Before you decide you have a "Straight" in your hands be very sure your reading technique is correct. This person is motivated by his sense of duty and ethics. If he thinks he is right he will persist in the face of all odds. Albert Schweitzer or Davy Crockett are examples of such men. But this is not always good. It also produces crackpots who are sure their ideas are right and then proceed to force them on others. There is no doubt the Inquisition was led by one or more "Straights".

The Tip

Tip Up (also called Ski Jump): This designates a forward looking individual. He is the optimist, and for him the future is generally bright as he tends to create what he sees. Negative aspects in other parts of the reading can cloud this characteristic, but can never totally subdue it. Take it in to consideration when you see it.

Tip Down (also called The Hook): As might be expected this individual tends to the pessimistic. It is not as strong as other aspects, but it does color the reading.

Tip Straight (also known as the Straight Shot): This is the most common orientation, and is therefore neutral. It doesn't give any notable coloration to the reading. In the case where the Hang Straight is capped with a Straight Shot you have what is known as the "Straight Straight ". He has the Straight tendencies to the max. If you come across one of these know that you are holding the rarest of rares in your hands.

Degree: The characteristics associated with the hang are actually the result of a bending of the penis in one or more directions. In fact the Bent Penis, one of our major classifications, is simply an accentuated bending. Thus it becomes the major factor in the reading, and we have designated it as a separate type. In this special case one can generally identify the basic root type before the superposition of the bend. For a truly accurate reading the basic root type must be considered first, and then the bend.

The Erection

This most fascinating of all body functions, is also an important element in the interpretation of the reading. In fact a reading can be totally turned around if the aspects of the erection are significantly different from those of the flaccid state. It can be quite a surprise to think you have a genuine Nightstick in your hands only to find out upon erection that it is no longer than a decently engorged Pinky! There are numerous significant points to notice about the erection so we will explore them one at a time.

In general the erection reveals and clarifies the more subtle aspects of the man. It provides deeper penetration into hidden parts of the personality. Unapparent talents or insanities will show up here, as well as readings on levels of passion and energy. The erection is not something that the serious Genitologist ignores!

The Point

How's He Pointing?: That's right. Check the direction on that erection. Is he pointing right or left? Is he pointing in the same direction that he hangs? You may be surprised to find that he is not. This indicates a split in his personality. While socially he will manifest the characteristics of the way he hangs, when you get to know him well or he is under pressure, expect the reactions of the way he points. The significance of the direction of the Point is the same as the significance of the direction of the Hang. If he points in the direction he hangs you can expect him to be a very consistent fellow.

It is also important to note if he points up, out or down. Pointing up indicates a high energy passionate individual. In this particular aspect of Genitology one individual can vary from day to day. As his energy waxes and wanes so will his erection. It is the overall trend that has to be looked at here. To be totally accurate one would have to check the erection over several days. Is he most often pointing up? Then you can expect he is generally energetic.

If he points out then he is the steady on type, and if he is usually found pointing down then expect him to be slow. If it barely rises above the Hang he is a real slug.

Angle of Dangle

For those seeking the highest degrees of accuracy in their readings we now mention the "angle of the dangle" (as it is known in Genitological technical circles). This requires a protractor. You are trying to determine the angle of the Hang (flaccid state) in relationship to the angle of the Point (erect state). For example: if he points further left than he hangs, then the characteristics are more pronounced. On the other hand if he hangs further left than he points (erection is straighter) then the Hang Left characteristics would be diminished. Thus the expert also records the "angles of the dangles".

The Head

The head is another important feature of the erection. Watch carefully as the penis erects. Does the head flare out and get significantly larger as it grows? Know you have a real "hot head". This guy is very passionate, and highly excitable. Interestingly, it has been noticed that during the full moon the head flares even more on erection. As the head flares less so goes the passion. Although it might seem impossible, one case has been observed where the head remained the same size upon erection. You could bet that this guy was a real dud in bed and sure enough he was about as passionate as a cold noodle.

Class Changes

One of the more important considerations in the reading of the erection is the actual change in size from the flaccid to the fully erect penis. Actually this is crucial. As the picture in Fig. 6 illustrates, a small Pinky has swollen to the size of a large Nightstick! Although this is highly unusual it is not unknown. In fact this individual was quite an interesting study. On the surface he looked like the standard Pinky, and on casual observation

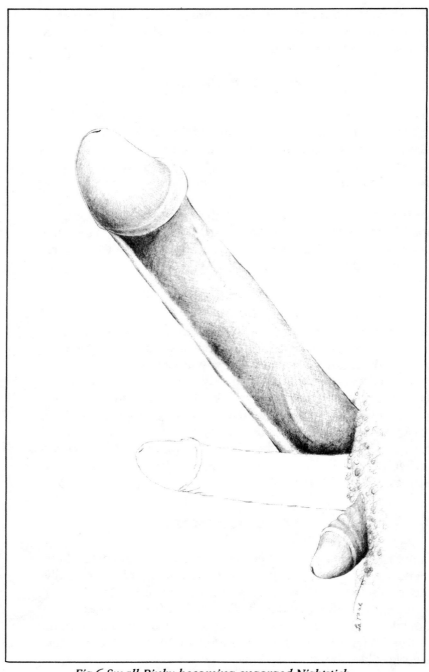

Fig.6 Small Pinky becoming engorged Nightstick.

people could not understand how this man had risen to chairmanship of one of the largest corporations in America. It was the erection that told the tale. Beneath his apparent mild exterior this man was a veritable bull. There is a lesson here. By taking note of the erect penis we discovered vital data that explained the apparent anomaly between his Pinky and his position in life.

With the above in mind let us take a look at all of the possible relationships between the flaccid and erect penis.

Change in size only: This is the most common case. The erect penis is just a larger version of the flaccid penis. The question here is; for any given penis type what is the size of the average erection? Unfortunately this is an area that requires some experience. Given this experience the Genitologist can then say if the erection is smaller or larger than normal. A smaller than normal erection signifies that the man lacks a bit in will power, and conversely a larger erection indicates greater will power.

Change in Class: Now the case also occurs where the erection is SO much larger that it actually throws it over into another Class. This is much rarer, and is essentially the case that we discussed above.

Radical Class Changes: Finally you get the extremely rare case where one sees a radical type change. We illustrate one possible example of this phenomenon, (Fig.7). This is a case where the Princely Pistol takes on the characteristics of the Toad Stool upon erection. Essentially what is seen here is a Dr. Jekyll, Mr. Hyde situation. If you ever see this phenomemon take close note of the types. If you're around him long enough you'll see him flip flop between the two personalities.

Proportions—Head/Shaft

After determining if there is any class change we need to do a more detailed examination to answer the following question: Do the proportions of the head compared to the shaft change upon erection? It is important then that good notes be taken on the size

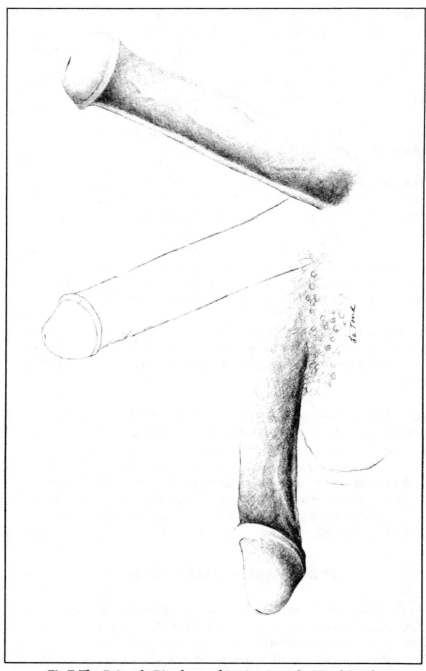

Fig.7 The Princely Pistol transforming into the Toad Stool.

and proportions before the penis is erected, because it is often messy getting rid of the erection once produced. In fact some Genitologists find it difficult to get a second reading, so get what you can while the getting is good.

If the head shrinks in proportion to the shaft it should make you leery. This guy is a braggert. He'll boast about his passionateness and whisper what he is going to do in you ear, but when it comes down to delivery he falls short.

Now if that head swells and grows proportionately larger than the shaft get ready for a wild ride. This guy will underestimate himself, but when he gets going he really gets going.

Finally if the proportions remain the same what you see is what you get.

As an added note we have yet to see a penis that shrinks upon erection. If you ever see one please call us collect with all the details.

Erectional analysis requires experience. So don't be dismayed if your first attempts are not perfect. We recommend viewing as many erect penises as possible to acquire expertise.

The
Nightstick

The Nightstick

OCCIDENTAL NAME

The Cock

ORIENTAL NAME

Long Thick Shaft—Large Head Flared

Personality Characteristics: If you believed most stories, you would think that women look on this type as the "Cadillac of Cocks". This long honkin' dong has been the subject of many books and movies, Harry Reems being a prime example. But on the contrary this is not true for most women. They prefer a little sensitivity along with the masculinity.

This is the macho type, ranging from the true macho to the pretended macho. On the outside you have the brutish athlete, the killer football player, the fraternity jock, and plunderer of young female cheerleaders. This is your true "party animal". Naturally he drinks beer and lots of it. In later years this can lead to the proverbial "beer gut".

Interestingly if he has intelligence he will come up successful in life. The domineering personality wins out because he knows what he wants and he knows what he wants is right. He can be a strong leader and may be found heading up his own business.

If he's the complete animal, over the years his beer gut will grow larger and his circle of friends smaller. You will find him on Sundays planted in front of the TV with his wide expanse of gut hanging out from beneath a soiled T-shirt, beer in hand. Thus we have the transformation of the animal athlete to the age-old slob.

Possible Nightsticks: Douglas Fairbanks, Mean Joe Green, Alexander Haig, Sylvester Stallone, Ernest Hemmingway, John Wayne, Bluto, John Belushi, Bullwinkle, and Chris Pressler.

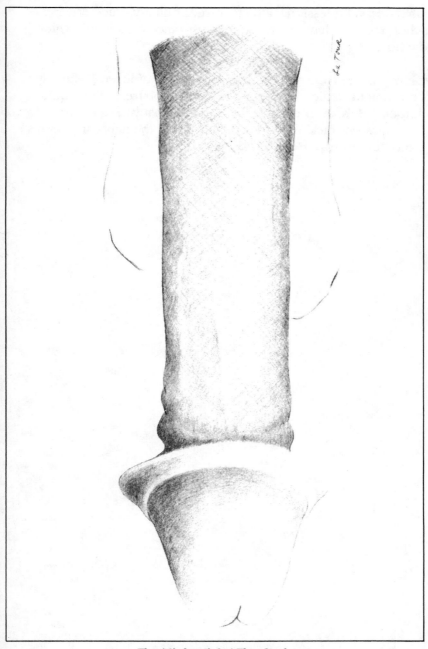

The Nightstick / The Cock
This is the macho type, ranging from the true macho
to the pretended macho.

Professions: Professional athlete, career military, truck driver, butcher, independent business man, insurance broker, and game show host.

Type of Lover: He is your macho manly type of lover. Definitely not a romantic, ladies. You're more likely to be treated to a quick in and out. He's an insensitive lover, but if what you're interested in is a quick hot fuck, this is it. For him when the lights are out it's just another fast trip. He is a real hot rod.

Le
Long
Carabine

Le Long Carabine
OCCIDENTAL NAME

The Shaft
ORIENTAL NAME

Long Thin Shaft—Pointed Head

Personality Characteristics: For this guy "playboy" is the name of the game. He's smooth talking, and has been known to talk his way into or out of anything. Naturally he's good looking, with straight teeth (but a crooked smile). He's so cool, he's so right. Dressing straight out of GQ, you could almost take him for a mannequin. Perfect right down to his French bikini underwear. He spends beyond his means because for him money is just a means to an end. And women are usually the end.

For the true Long Carabine pussy is the end all and be all of existence. He's actually the classic MCP (Male Chauvinist Pig), but he's such a smooth pig that the women don't seem to notice, or maybe they just don't care. When he directs his attention her way she forgets all about the stories she's heard from her girlfriends and proceeds to melt all over him. She thinks somehow for her it will be different. He's charming, he's attentive, and she's sure he's never been smitten with anybody as he seems to be smitten with her. Sorry but this is the original classic love 'em and leave 'em guy. He's enamored with women in general, and his goal is to have all of them. In fact, it has been proven by extensive surveying that more woman lose their virginity to Le Long Carabine than any other type.

As a side note, men have to watch themselves a bit with the Shaft. This smooth slick guy can be devastating in the business and political world. As a manipulator of people and situations to gain advantage, he is the master. They had him in mind when they coined the phrase "he got shafted".

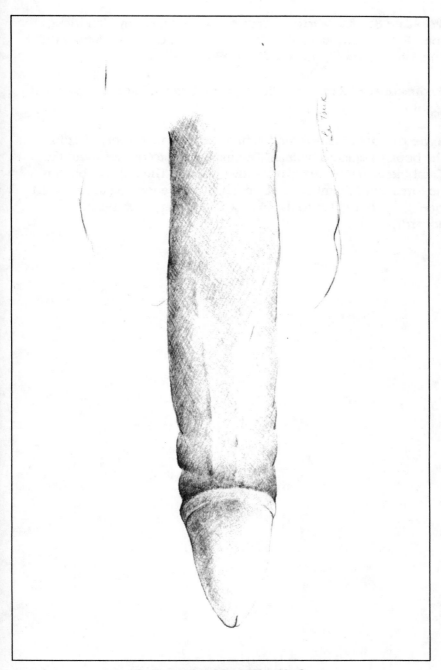

The Long Carabine / The Shaft
For this guy "playboy" is the name of the game.

Possible Shafts: Warren Beatty, Clark Gable, Jimmy Hendricks, John F. Kennedy, Richard Burton, Don Juan, Casanova, Sitting Bull (not often known), Louis XIV, and Woody Allen.

Professions: PR man, politician, lawyer, agent, salesman, actor, gigolo.

Type of Lover: This is Mr. Technique. He knows every trick in the book to satisfy a woman. The main thing to realize about the Carabine is that he really does love women. The only problem is he loves all of them! So ladies if what you are looking for is a wild ride, give your ticket to the man with Le Long Carabine. All aboard!

The
Dented
Dick

The Dented Dick

OCCIDENTAL NAME

The Crank

ORIENTAL NAME

Bent Penis

Personality Characteristics: He is your basic oddball. He's kinky. You'll find most of your S&M, bondage, B&D, and the rest of the unusual sexual practices favored by the man with the Dented Dick. Sometimes it isn't very obvious but a close inspection will show the kink. So if at all in doubt do a thorough inspection. Now of course the kink isn't necessarily bad. Indeed variety can be the spice of life, and if you're bored this might be just the fling for you. With him it will always be interesting.

On a wider scale he tends to think and act differently from the crowd. You know—the bozo who ends up drunk and streaks the party, or the guy who tells off color jokes at the president's daughter's debutante debut. Deep down he's looking for the kick in life, looking for new and different experiences, and especially he's looking for the shock value. They can be some of the funniest people you've ever met.

Many times the Crank will end up in show business as one of those zany comedians. If you haven't guessed already, Lenny Bruce is in the Dented Dick Hall of Fame. Dented Dicks exhibit several distinct personality types. There is the extremely outgoing type that doesn't give a fuck what others think about him, and then there is the "Closet Kink". This is the guy that mumbles "Want some candy little girl?", and hides in dark alleys. He is also the true master of perversion, and a peek into his bedroom can be horrifying or exciting depending on your bent.

All in all The Crank is the rarest type, and also the most varied. This is because the bend can be superimposed on all the other penis types. It is important to consider then the native penis type

48

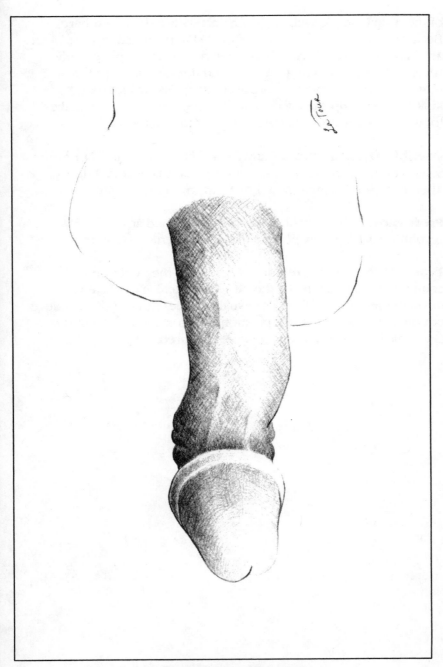

The Dented Dick / The Crank
He is your basic oddball. He's kinky.

of the individual, as well as the characteristics described here. Because of this, interpretation of the D.D. still remains more of an art than a science. Obviously our research is incomplete. Only recently have we begun to understand the variations. In the near future we will be able to more accurately classify him based on: kink left, right, up or down, as well as degree of kink. He makes for a fascinating study that we're bound to pursue.

Possible Dented Dicks: Daffy Duck (the archetypal D.D.), Soupy Sales, Lenny Bruce, Rasputin, Van Gogh, H.P. Lovecraft, Edgar Allen Poe, Sun Young Moon, Edi Amin, and Frazer Smith.

Professions: Show business (especially comedians), revolutionaries, gurus, political activists, inventors, writers.

Type of Lover: If you're out to explore all the nooks and crannies of sex, he'll make the perfect guide. He can take you through the full side show of sexual fantasies, special devices, love potions, new positions, old positions—you name it he knows it. Girls this is a red hot number so be prepared.

The
Princely
Pistol

The Princely Pistol

OCCIDENTAL NAME

The Wand

ORIENTAL NAME

Long Thin Shaft—Large Head Flared

Personality Characteristics: Aesthetic, sensuous, a great lover, but not always practical in the real world; these are the attributes of the Pistol. He's a mystic, a dreamer, and often psychic, and if the penis is well aspected he can carry his dreams into reality. He's an adventurer, seeking new experiences in his mind or in the world. Many great artists and architects fall in this class.

At his worst the Pistol can be quite a disaster. The guy who talks a good game but never actually does anything. The daydreamer who walks through life in a fog, never really taking hold of it. But in all this mist, he is always the romantic. Take note ladies, although he may seem the perfect mate, he's generally not very stable. If what you want is kids and a husband and the paycheck every other Friday then you had better forget the Pistol. If you are willing to put up with his spur of the moment trips and his spur of the moment ideas then he may be the white knight of your dreams. He likes having a playmate be it in bed or in business.

The overall impression of the Princely Pistol seems rather genteel and mild. But in actuality he has another side to him— bullheadedness. He wants to do things his way, and although he is nice about it he'll have it his way or not at all. His intelligence can get him through these situations without creating a scene. Unfortunately at times that same intelligence fails to penetrate the problems of his own life, leaving them unsolved. The Pistol lacks persistence more than any other quality, but with it he can do anything.

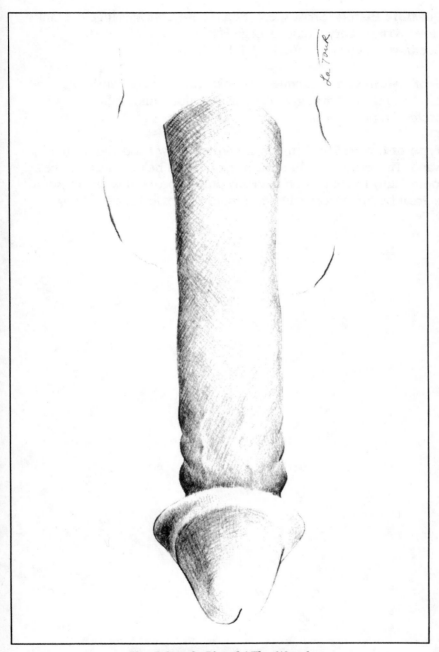

The Princely Pistol / The Wand
Aesthetic, sensuous, a great lover, but not always practical
in the real world.

Possible Pistols: Shakespere, Edgar Casey, Michaelangelo, Frank Lloyd Wright, Cary Grant, George Harrison, The Maharishi, Beethoven, Schroder, and Rudolph Valentino.

Professions: Artist, architect, counsellor, minister, musician, psychic, gigolo, actor, gambler, airline pilot, philosopher, professor, poet.

Type of Lover: This is the man with the slow hand and magic wand. The ladies love him. He's smooth and he's sensual and he's more likely to get you off than any other type. So if what you want is great bedtime stories he's a spinner of magical tales.

The
Spike

The Stogey
OCCIDENTAL NAME

The Spike
ORIENTAL NAME

Short Thick Shaft—Pointed Head

Personality Characteristics: This is the little tough guy. The Banty Rooster. Street wise, overbearing, at times pushy. You'll often find him with a large stogey stuck in the side of his face. There is always a bit of "prove himself" in his actions. The Spike can be a reliable hard worker, or the boastful braggart hanging out at the pool hall or gym. He likes to keep himself in good shape and is generally muscular with a tight little rock hard ass.

He's trying to project a manly image and it shows in his cars and clothes. You'll often see him hunkered down behind the wheel of a mean machine with his girlfriend draped over his shoulder. His clothes also reflect that manly look whether it be black leather jackets, disco stud, or immaculate three piece suits with a fedora hat cocked over one eye.

He's got a strong "come on" with the women, as much to impress the guys as the woman he's chasing down. Although when he gets her in bed she may be surprised. If he trusts her he can be quite gentle and caring. And once he's married he can make an excellent husband who really loves his wife and kids. But frankly, though you'd never get him to admit it, he'd rather hang out with the boys.

In his career he seems to gravitate towards power positions. Although he is apparently seeking power it's actually admiration he desires. And you can see this quality from the union organizer to the politican.

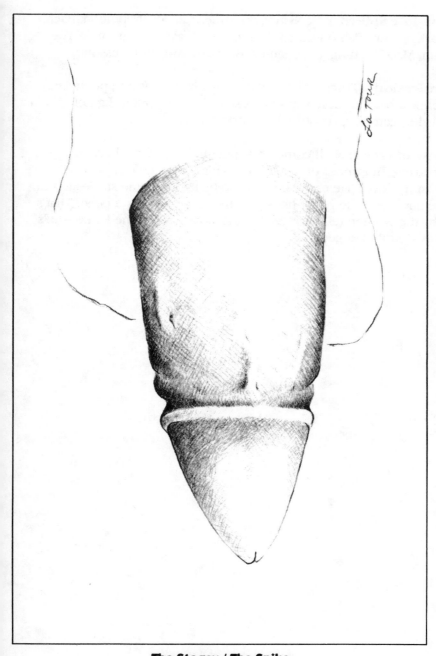

The Stogey / The Spike
The little tough guy. He can be a reliable hard worker, or the boastful braggart hanging out at the pool hall.

Possible Spikes: Jack Nicholson, James Cagney, Napoleon, Bach, Mark Antony, Pablo Picasso, Humphrey Bogart Caesar, Attila The Hun, Mao Tse-tung, Jesse James, Billy The Kid, and Mussolini.

Professions: Truck driver, union organizer, gangster, politician, political boss, undercover cop, assembly line worker, fighter, pool hustler, gambler, construction worker, lawyer.

Type of Lover: He'll come on super studly, and might seem uncaring. But once you get to know him, girls, he can be a sensitive lover. He can make love so he'll have some stories to tell the guys, or, if he really likes you, they'll never hear a peep. That's why the women tell such conflicting stories about the Spike—he's truly doubled edged.

The
Toad Stool

The Putz
OCCIDENTAL NAME

The Toad Stool
ORIENTAL NAME

Short Thin Shaft—Flat Head

Personality Characteristics: The Toad Stool (also affectionately known as Toady) is often weak. He can be immediately spotted with his cold clammy hand shake, flabby body, pale white skin, and '50's crew cut or long hippie hair (depending on his leanings.) Generally a man of amazing intellegence in some areas, he can be shockingly stupid when it comes to dealing with areas such as women, parties, and general socializing. The term "nerd" has been widely used to describe such a fellow.

While apparently innocuous, the Toady is actually quite lecherous. Possibly this accounts for his seeking jobs in colleges where he can prey on innocent young college girls. Bedazzled by the glamor of college life and college professors these girls tend to overlook his shortcomings.

The Putz seems to fall into two different classes, depending on how flared his flat head is. The first, being the less flared, could give a hoot for socializing and people in general. This is your Nobel Prize winner, your dedicated scientist, engineer or medical researcher. His life revolves around his work and he wouldn't have it any other way.

The second type (more flared) wants to be in the swing, but fails madly. He tends to become the psychologist or professor. These professions give him a certain altitude making it easier to be "in". It also makes him a pompous ass as he is so insecure. In this case we have found no more appropriate description—a short thin shafted flat headed cock.

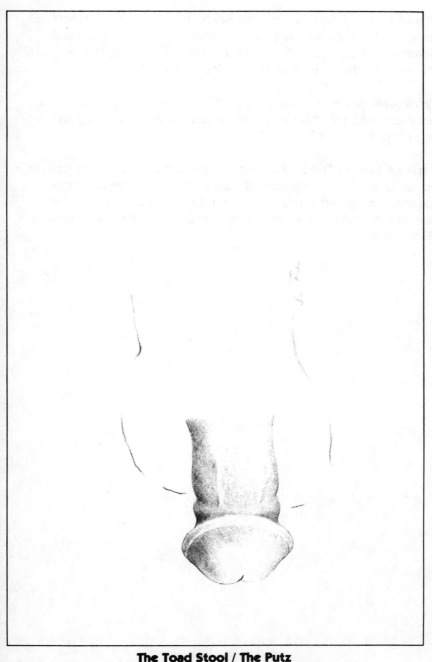

The Toad Stool / The Putz
Generally amazingly intellegent, he can be shockingly stupid when it comes to dealing with women, parties, and general socializing.

Possible Toad Stools: Genghis Kahn, Alfred Hitchcock (there is some controversy whether he was really a Nightstick), Richard Nixon, Mr. Wizard, Alfalfa, Sigmund Freud, Karl Jung, Pavlov, Walter Mitty, Boris Karloff, Stan Laurel, and Curly.

Professions: Doctor, scientist, professor, psychologist (can be a sex therapist), psychiatrist, psychoanalyist, electronics engineer, egg head.

Type of Lover: The initial reaction would be to leave this section blank. Really he is not much of a lover. Watching the late night horror movies and eating crackers in bed is more his style. He does get it up, but he is also known as the master of premature ejaculation.

The
Pinky

The Pinky

The Bamboo Shoot

Short Thin Shaft—Small Head

Personality Characteristics: When it comes to sexuality this man is a limp lizard. As far as the Pinky is concerned that thing between his legs is to relieve the pressure in his bladder. We wish you luck in getting it up, ladies. And when you do get it up you'll probably wonder why you even bothered. Many women have been known to remark "Where is it, is it in yet?"

Not surprisingly this doesn't bother the Pinky. He's lost in another world, figuring equations or calculating how many years we have until the universe ends. He doesn't understand much about sex, and frankly could care less.

The Pinky is the antithesis of the Nightstick, all head—no rod. He's a bookworm, a professor, an economist, a computernick, in short an egghead. His idea of fashion can be found in the 1953 Reader's Digest "Who's Who in the Farm Belt."

Probably his most notable trait is his minimal awareness of the world around him. Pinky's are nearsighted to a man. With thick hornrimmed glasses and thinning hair, he stands before his classes spouting what to him is perfect sense while his students snore. In one recorded instance a Pinky bounced off a pair of 38 D's, mumbled something and walked off, his nose never having left the book.

When his wife asks for a divorce he's generally incredulous. He thought everything was just great! Simply said this man doesn't know a pussy from a hole in the ground. Despite their faults, Pinky's are hard working and if a woman wants a good provider (and not much else) the Pinky is the perfect mate.

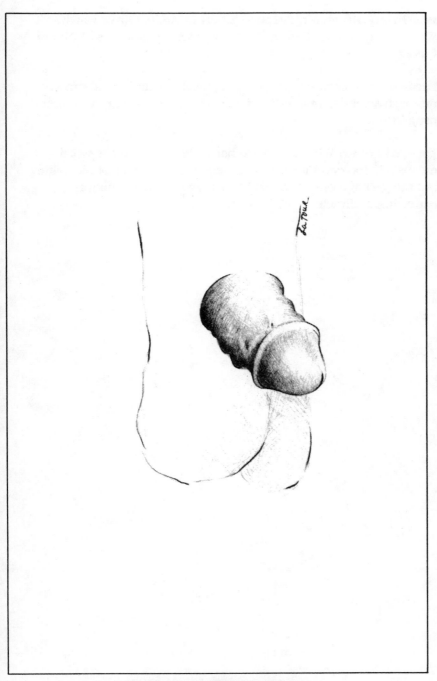

The Pinky / The Bamboo Shoot
The Pinky is the antithesis of the Nightstick, all head—no rod.

Possible Pinkys: Mr. Peepers, Albert Einstein, Oliver Hardy, Walter Mitty, Jimmy Carter, Porky Pig, Don Quixote, and Colonel Custer .

Professions: Professor, economist, legal researcher, laboratory research scientist, mathematician, orchestra musician, computer programmer.

Type of Lover: What lover? He hardly knows what the word means. He looks on it more as a necessary task, sort of like taking out the garbage once a week. Ladies, expecting anything is expecting a miracle.

The
Pud
(Big Daddy)

The Pud
OCCIDENTAL NAME

The Dork
ORIENTAL NAME

Short Thick Shaft—Large Head Flared

Personality Characteristics: A little over weight, verging on the pudgy, you can spot the Big Daddy by the swagger in his walk. People think of him as either a relentless worker or a pompous asshole—he could care less. As long as he is in control there is no problem. He doesn't give a damn for people's feelings, just getting the job done. The Dork can be an efficient office manager, or the loud, boisterous guy in the bar with his buttocks hanging over the stool. You can call him a boor, brutish, and ill-mannered, but his ballsy certainty and determination has gotten him through many a hard time where others would have quit. He's a hard driving man. In many ways the society rests on such men's shoulders.

Ladies, you can bet with those characteristics he won't make much of a romantic. He's not likely to court you with subtleties—poetry and candlelight. He's more likely to entrance you with a fat wad of bills, then hustle you off to the hotel in his Cadillac. If he likes you he will put you up, and get you whatever you want. But beware, if you try to get the upper hand he'll throw you out or knock you out. You'll always have to be subservient to the Big Daddy.

Possible Dorks: Orson Wells, Henry VIII, Archie Bunker, Kruschev, Peter Ustinov, Winston Churchill, Teddy Roosevelt, Broderick Crawford.

Professions: Butcher, politician, truck driver, policeman, stockbroker, office manager, or anywhere he can be "the boss".

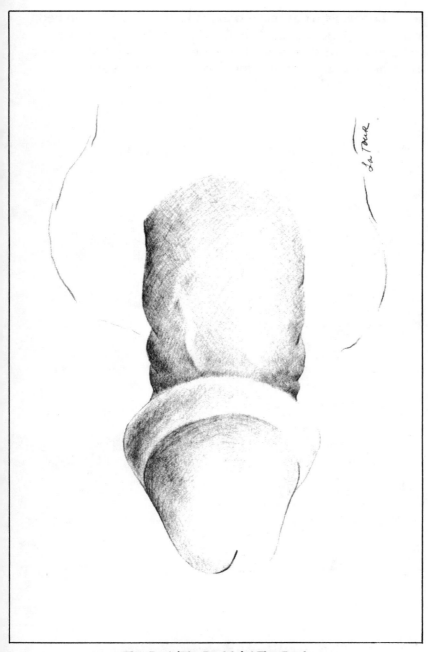

The Pud (Big Daddy) / The Dork
The efficient office manager, or the loud, boisterous guy in the bar with
his buttocks hanging over the stool.

Type of Lover: Don't expect too much ladies. He's a bull in bed, slow and strong, but definitely unimaginative. The Dork is the classic example: he'll be making love one minute, and rolled over snoring the next. Incidentally don't ever try to get on top.

The
Passion
Flower

The Passion Flower

We now take up the "flower of humanity", the ladies of the world and their wonderful Passion Flower. The Flower is generally considered mysterious by both men and women, and has been since the dawn of time. Unlike the Joystick it doesn't present itself readily to the world. One has to be willing to probe a bit to discover its secrets.

When you first approach this subject the Jade Gates will not be in full view. You will be greeted by the muff, and indeed it has some bearing on the subject at hand.

The muff has a lot to do with the robustness of the personality you are about to plumb. Color is a minor factor in your determination, although lighter colors do tend to be a bit less robust. Far more important is the density. If an ant in the muff were to feel he was lost in the Amazon jungle, this would indicate very hearty characteristics. A sparse bush denotes a more ethereal personality type.

As you delve a bit deeper you will come upon the Passion Flower. It is composed of the majora (outer lips), the minora (inner lips), and the clitoris. The clit is important enough that we handle it separately in the next section.

The Majora

The outer lips of the Flower can range from thick fleshy mounds to thin taut bumps. We have found that the majora presents a glimpse into the inner nature of the woman. Her strength of character and the degree of personal certainty will be reflected in the size of the majora. A large fleshy majora indicates that this lady has a sense of herself and an appreciation for her self worth. The small majora will not be strong and generally seeks support from a man, or tries to retire from the world altogether.

72

The Minora

The minora generally defines the degree of outgoingness and sophistication of the lady involved. The larger the minora the coarser the lady tends to be. She's also more sexually oriented. This woman won't be shy, and if she likes you she might just come right up and say so. If you get an outright proposition be assured she is large in the minora.

Conversely, if her minora is smaller she will be more sophisticated—looking for the "finer" things in life. She is the more delicate personality, with a finely attuned awareness and perception of life and people. She'll have to be interested in you before you can interest her in the bedroom. And if you want her you'll have to go get her.

Other Factors

There are several other characteristics to take into consideration in the reading.

The color of the pussy is an indicator of the passion level of the Passion Flower. The very pale pink indicates a feeble ardor, while the rosy red pussy is a flower that is always ready to bloom. This is also an indicator of the lady's emotional propensities.

There are other qualities even more difficult to classify. These attributes comprise categories of odd or unusual markings and convolutions. Even now hot debate rages in Genitological circles as to their meanings.

Each female pussy is uniquely different. The convolutions of the labia form a singular pattern from woman to woman. There is no doubt that if one could totally understand all the nuances one would have a complete picture of the woman. On the other hand the variety here is so tremendous that most professional Genitologists agree that it is impossible to categorize all the details.

Nevertheless research continues in this fascinating area, and a few tentative conclusions can be drawn. If a specific zone of the pussy, be it the labia or the clit, is detailed with unusual markings, or is unusually convoluted, that zone figures more prominently in the reading.

Cases of special markings are extremely rare, and the conclusions drawn at this time are purely hypothetical. One investigator turned up a highly unusual case of a woman having a freckled clit. Further investigation revealed that the woman's clitoris was extremely sensitive, and upon stimulation the researcher was able to count nineteen distinct orgasms in a five minute period. There is no doubt that the clit was emphasized in this woman, and one may assume that the freckled markings were indicative of the extraordinary condition of her clitoris.

As careful researchers we cannot feel justified in drawing a broad conclusion from a single observation. We can only say that unusual markings or convolutions tend to indicate a greater emphasis on those parts of the pussy affected.

The Jewel

Although the clitoris is tiny, it has received the lion's share of attention in the past few years, and it plays an important part in Genitology. Its function in the reading is similar to that of the erection. The clitoris is a modifier and its aspects color the reading.

As with the penis you will want to observe this little jewel in the aroused and unaroused state.

The Sleeping Jewel

After the basic reading to determine the type of pussy you have in front of you, gently move the labia aside to get a good look at that baby. Observe whether it is large or small, hidden away in its hood or standing right out in the open.

The size of the clit determines the degree of passion of the lady. The larger her clit the greater her ardor. The more the clitoris is exposed the more readily she will exhibit her passion. For instance Big Mamas often have a large protruding clit which matches their boisterous upfront sexuality. The Rosebud on the other hand tends to a small hidden clit which is manifested in her reserve.

Awakening The Jewel

Now wet your finger and gently stroke the clitoris. Or use the tongue which is highly recommended. Get her good and hot. Observe the change in the clit as things get more lively. The Jewel will enlarge, and may protrude from its hood. These are the signs you are looking for.

The degree of enlargement is important. Does she go from an almost tiny speck to a huge swollen gland? (Fig.8) Get ready for the time of your life. This girl could tear your root off. Similarly, if the clit was hidden but now stands smartly at attention she will be reserved in the beginning, but ardent by night's end.

Fig.8 Rosebud's tiny clitoris swelling to
a magnificent huge gland upon stimulation.

If the clit is hidden and remains hidden be assured there are some intentions here which she is not airing. You will probably find it difficult to get her off, as she is hiding something. She's not what you'd call your upfront lady.

If you get no engorgement at all just pack it in for the night and go home.

Once again remember this is a sensitive area and it requires a fine touch and delicate technique to correctly interpret the signs. Don't be concerned if your first readings don't come out well. Practice makes perfect.

The
Lady Finger

The Lady Finger
OCCIDENTAL NAME,

The Pearl
ORIENTAL NAME

Large Majora—Small Minora

Personality Characteristics: This is the sophisticated lady, or at least she aspires to it. She can be dainty or she can be matronly. She can be a truly artistic and intellectual sophisticate, or just a pretender to the throne. Make no mistake, she knows what she wants in either case. But pulling it off can be another story.

No matter what her station in life, you'll know the Pearl as she's always doing her best to be elegant and graceful. Unfortunately this can leave her open to social embarrassment. Nothing could be more horrifying to the aspiring Pearl than to find a piece of spinach glued to her front tooth after a night on the town. It is interesting to note that if the Lady Finger can come to laugh at herself she can become quite a comedienne. Often the combination of bumbling and elegance is quite funny.

If you meet a witty intelligent lady the chances are that if you look between her legs you will find the Pearl. Career women fall in this category, generally purposeful and moving forward in life. You'll have to be moving pretty fast yourself to catch her. When carried to extremes she can be stuffy and snooty, very much above the "Hoi Polloi".

Like the pearl her sensual nature can be soft and lustrous or cold and hard. It's all in the way you handle her.

Possible Pearls: Diana Ross, Queen Elizabeth, Madame Curie, Ayn Rand, Pearl Buck, Jackie Onassis, Katherine Hepburn, Jane Fonda, Nancy Reagan, "Madame", and Helen of Troy.

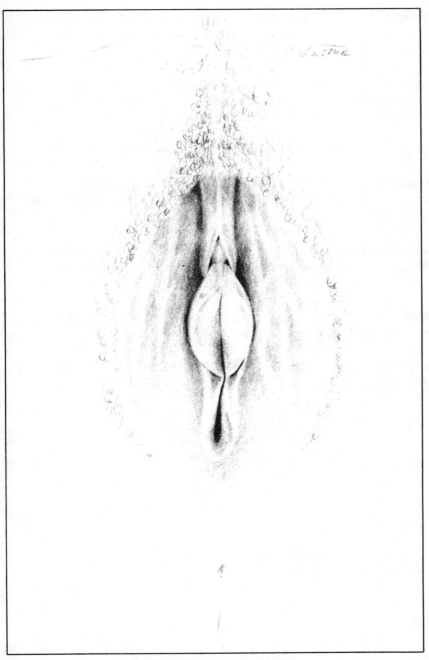

The Lady Finger / The Pearl
This is the sophisticated lady.

Professions: Lawyer, executive, executive secretary, entertainer, politician, wife of a politician, hostess, high class call girl, fashion model, and artist.

Type of Lover: This is your knowledgeable, cosmopolitan, sophisticated lover. Catch her in her late 20's and early 30's after she has really bloomed. She can be very creative.

Clitoral Aspects of The Lady Finger

Hidden Clit: This aspect pushes her toward coolness. In its extreme it could have been the model for the saying "Colder than a witch's tit".

Protruding Clit: This is the sophisticated seducer. She is the older woman who loves to seduce young men. Mrs. Robinson (The Graduate) loved her young lollipop.

Small Clit: This makes her dainty and delicate physically and emotionally. This type definitely needs a slow hand.

Large Clit: She's aggressive. She's the executive type. This lady will make every effort to control the relationship.

The
Big Mama

Big Mama
OCCIDENTAL NAME

The Mouth
ORIENTAL NAME

Large Majora—Small Minora

Personality Characteristics: The Big Mama lives up to her name. Her prime characteristic is openness and it manifests itself in various ways.

She can be funloving and loud, or brash, obnoxious and loud. But note, she is always loud. Flashy, wearing outrageous clothes or just colorful, it is her nature to be the center of attention.

She is a gossiper—hanging over a fence, cigarette dangling from her lips, diet soda in hand spreading the latest dirt. She has a loud unmistakable laugh which she uses to punctuate her remarks. The Mouth is always on a diet, coming off a diet or getting ready to start a new diet.

She is a very strong woman and given the right environment and motivation she can really get things done. The people she works with will love her for it. She can set a real hardworking example or a real hard drinking example, because whatever she does she does it to the max. You'll like her or you'll hate her—nobody is neutral to the Big Mama.

Possible Mamas: Janis Joplin, Bette Midler, Queen Victoria, Catherine The Great, Golda Meyer, Barbara Walters, Lucy, Helen Wheels, The Virgin Mary, Mona Lisa, Miss Piggie and Bella Abzug.

Professions: The charity organizer, pushy mother, expert bridge player, waitress, bartender, madam, assembly line worker, keypunch operator, office manager and Congresswoman.

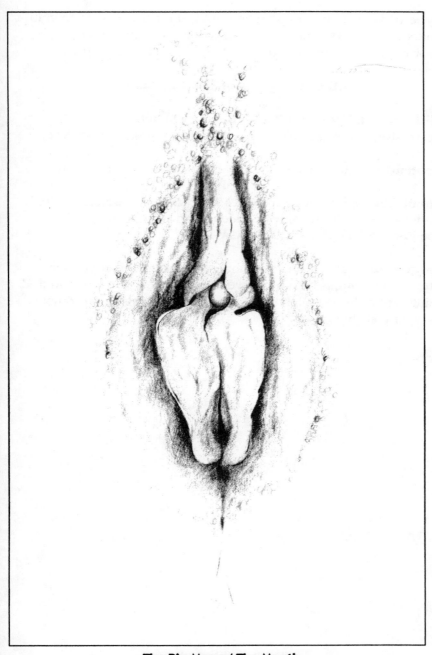

The Big Mama / The Mouth
She can be funloving and loud, or brash, obnoxious and loud. But note,
she is always loud.

Type of Lover: She's brash. She's bold. She's just as likely to grab yours as you are to grab hers. So if you are looking for a rip snorting wild evening the best advice is: Grab it and hang on.

Clitoral Aspects of The Big Mama

Hidden Clit: The closet Big Mama. She will not be so overtly aggressive, but get her alone and there is no mistaking her type.

Protruding Clit: This is the Classic Big Mama in all her glory.

Small Clit: As the clit gets smaller The Mouth gets quieter. Make no mistake, she'll probably be louder than any one around her, she just won't be as loud as the Classic.

Large Clit: To this Mama everything has to be done larger than life. If something is wrong believe me you'll hear about it. And if things are right you might find yourself in the biggest impromptu party of your life.

The
Prissy Pussy

The Prissy Pussy

OCCIDENTAL NAME

The Rosebud

ORIENTAL NAME

Small Majora—Small Minora

Personality Characteristics: You've seen this one. Pursed lips and the hair pulled back in a bun. Clothes from the 1950's, mid-calf plaid skirts, nylons with the seam in the back, and white blouses. And don't forget the sour look on her puss. Her body tends to be neat and well groomed. She's very proper, some would call it fussy.

Given some authority the Rosebud can be devastating. You may have run into her in the school library, or (heaven forbid) she was your second grade teacher. Not very nice to kids. But if her pussy is modified by an auspicious clitoral aspect she can turn out to be the nice old lady down the street who hands out cookies.

Amazingly, although you wouldn't believe it, she has a romantic side. If you could peek under her bed you'd find a pile of Harlequin romances. But this is all in her fantasy world. In fact study has shown that the majority of old maids are Prissy Pussies. If she does marry it will probably be to a similarly unsexy fellow, such as the Pinky, and he'll be henpecked at that.

Possible Prissy Pussies: Pat Nixon, Jane Austin, Abigail Van Buren, Amy Vanderbilt, Olive Oil, Dr. Joyce Brothers, Emily Post, and Emily Dickenson.

Professions: Teacher, librarian, author, legal secretary, dean of women, salvation army band member, scientist, and nun. (Note: this type has never been seen selling used cars.)

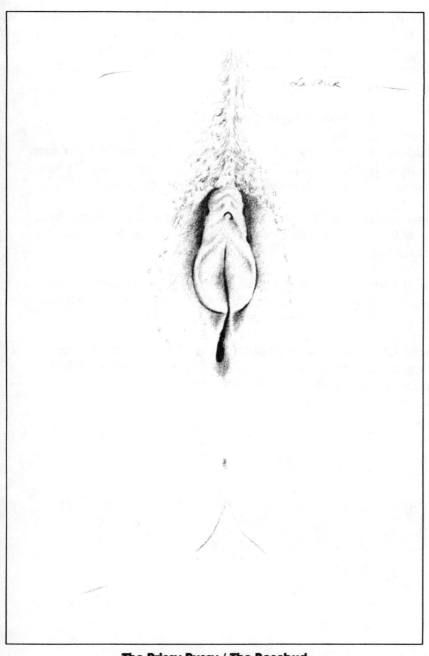

The Prissy Pussy / The Rosebud
The lady that made the rules for the Victorian Era was
definitely a Rosebud.

Type of Lover: Her pucker can be dispassionate to say the least. The lady that made the rules for the Victorian era was definitely a Prissy Pussy. You know the line, "Men are horny beasts but it is our duty to put up with their sexual necessities...once a month. Just think of something else, dear".

Clitoral Aspects of The Prissy Pussy

Hidden Clit: This is the absolute epitomy of unsexiness. No need to spread her legs to find out. She looks like she's always sucking on a lemon. She is where the term sour puss originated.

Protruding Clit: This will bring to the Bud a bit of a blossom. She will tend toward the petite pretty side, and be more cheerful and friendly.

Small Clit: This is your basic librarian. You know, hair bun, thick glasses, the works. You can often find her browsing through bus, plane, and train schedules, as well as phone books.

Large Clit: She is the most outgoing of all Rosebuds. This aspect brings a warmth to the otherwise cool Bud. A large clitted Bud has even been known to tell an off colored joke!

The
Venus
Man Trap

The Venus Man Trap

OCCIDENTAL NAME

The Butterfly

ORIENTAL NAME

Prickus Teasus

Scientific Name

Small Majora—Large Minora

Personality Characteristics: This is the vamp, the enticer, the femme fatale. You can bet behind those cool sexy eyes she is always calculating. She may be figuring her next trick or how to get that man to pop the big question. You'll find her in tight jeans and tank tops or shimmery dresses slit to the hip. Her body is bait, she knows it, she uses it. This is the original prick teaser, and you know she gets what she wants. She is vain about her body and usually keeps it in good shape. Occasionally if the Butterfly spends too much time in bars she'll get sloppy as she grows older. It is quite a shock when the old wiles don't work as well as they used to. Aging is worse than the plague.

Professionally she is a prostitute at worst, at her best a glamorous movie star loved by all. She also can be found at home in front of the TV set watching the soaps eating bon-bons. Bosses love to put her out front as the secretary (she makes delicious window dressing). And occasionally when her crafty mind turns to business she can be a very shrewd executive, business woman, or an excellent saleswoman (expecially selling to men). In dealing with her you will have to remember she is always calculating. So unless you feel like Dick Butkus don't tackle the Butterfly, she is heavier than she looks.

Possible Venus Man Traps: Belle Starr, Mata Hari, Cleopatra, Greta Garbo, Mae West, Marilyn Monroe, Jane Mansfield, Pat Benatar, Scarlet O' Hara, Venus, and Theda Bara.

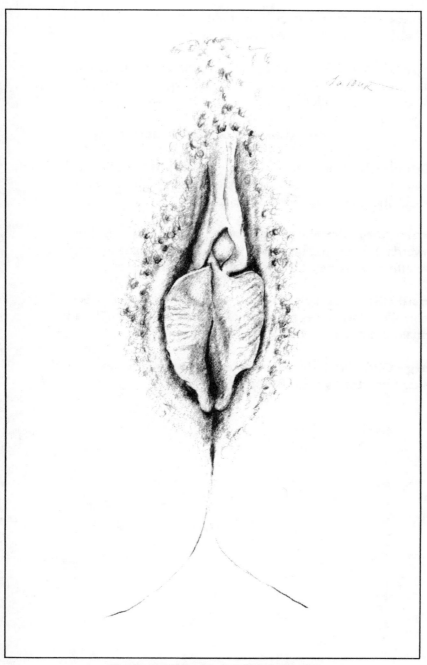

The Venus Man Trap / The Butterfly
This is the vamp, the enticer, the femme fatale.

Professions: Secretary, saleswomen, executive (rare), movie star, call girl, model, spy, singer, and stripper.

Type of Lover: She can be wild, passionate, and kinky, or calculatingly cool. This lady has the technique. Naturally, it's part of her stock in trade!

Clitoral Aspect of The Butterfly

Hidden Clit: Mata Hari is the epitome of this type. She is the true devious man trapper. For her sex is a weapon. In the extreme aspect she plays it purely for the game.

Protruding Clit: She is much more overtly sexy. Tending towards the gushing type. She will flaunt her sexuality, enjoying the effects it creates. Strippers often fall in to this category.

Small Clit: She is attractive and sexy, but her sexuality is well controlled. Her life is not totally focused on sex. You'll find female executives in this type.

Large Clit: The flashy, glamorous movie star. The sex symbol using her attractiveness for profit.

The
Slit

The Slit
OCCIDENTAL NAME

The Split Tail
ORIENTAL NAME

Small Majora—Minora almost not visible

Personality Characteristics: The name tells all here. She's a little girl. All little girls start out as Slits, but as they grow older they mature in to other types. Some never do. You've seen her—the innocent one. The one with the cutesy look on her face and little girl voice. When she wants something she'll preface it by looking up at you from under her shy lashes. What man can say no to the Slit? She might look innocent, but it is not always true. This Lolita can really surprise you, she may be truly innocent or an uninhibited wanton in bed. The Slit easily drives men wild as she seems to be a virgin, and what man isn't attracted by a virgin? She'll get eaten more often than most women. Men can't resist that innocent pink Slit.

The Slit is looking for "Daddy" in her relationships. She likes the strong domineering type, so if you want her, now you know what to do to get her. The Slit is not really career motivated. Unless you call trying to get firmly entrenched under a man's wing a career.

The interesting thing about the Slit is she can mature into another type at any time. Women as old as 25 have been known to suddenly change types over night and thus their whole life will shift to match their new vagina type. So don't marry her with the expectation of her remaining an innocent Slit forever.

Possible Slits: Judy Garland, Shirley Temple, Goldie Hawn, Alice In Wonderland, Joan of Arc, Juliet, Princess Di, Eve, Guinevere, and Lady Godiva.

Professions: Dumb blonde, cutesy secretary, helpless wife, groupie, actress, telephone operator, burger clerk, and manicurist.

96

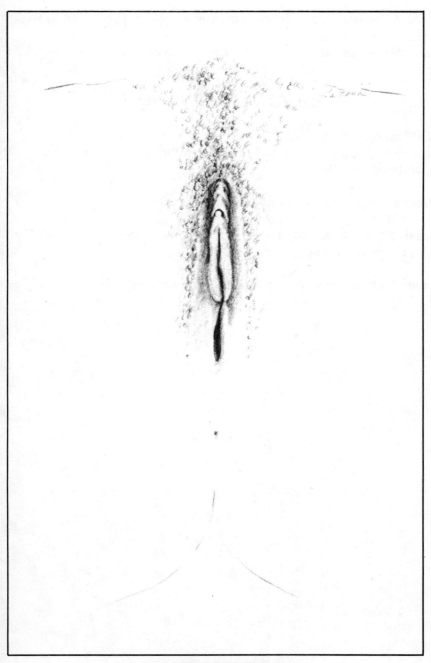

The Slit / The Split Tail
She is the little girl. All little girls start out as Slits.

Type of Lover: She appears to be a sweet young peach, but as we already mentioned this could be very deceiving. Given the right man she can be an absolute wild cat. And even better, if she is truly innocent the right love-teacher can make her into one.

Clitoral Aspects of The Slit

Hidden Clit: If this one tells you she is a virgin you better believe it. Having a hidden clit truly amplifies all the innocent qualities of the Slit.

Protruding Clit: She looks innocent but ain't.

Small Clit: A small clit on the Slit makes her very shy. It will take a lot to get her pussy purring.

Large Clit: If you've ever wanted an innocent wild virgin this is the one.

How To Do
A
Correct Reading

How To Do A Correct Reading

1. Get the tools you'll need: Pencil, Notebook, Wooden Ruler, Protractor (optional).

Preliminary Step

2. It is obvious that in order to do a reading at all you have to get the pants or panties off. Many techniques have been developed to accomplish this over the years. These have been well documented in prose, books and song as well as the common knowledge, so we won't cover it here. Take note though: as an official Genitological Researcher you now have another very effective technique—you're going to do a reading!

3. Most researchers prefer to do a reading after the subject has showered. Researchers are very dedicated people, and in most instances they have been known to shower with the subject to establish the rapport that is so important to a correct reading.

The Male

1. In the male reading first have him stand, feet a bit apart. Now grab that whanger and give it a good shaking out so that you get a true Hang. Be sure he is well dried so the penis isn't sticking at all. Note down the direction of the Hang. For more information on the Hang see "How's It Hanging?". Also get out the ruler and measure its lenght. (As a word of warning don't use a metal ruler—they can be cold, and you want your subject as comfortable as possible.) If you are going for the utmost in accuracy, pull out your protractor and measure the angle on his dangle. Note this down in the notebook.

2. Next get the subject into a comfortable position. Obviously this includes getting the legs well spread and the genitals exposed. Scrutinize that root. Take notes in your notebook on the following points: Is the head large or small? Flat, pointed, or flared? Check out the shaft. Is it long or short? Thick or thin? Is it bent, and if so

how much? Note all this down. Finally take a close look and see if there are any unusual markings or other interesting oddities. As a final warning here be sure to get this all down on paper. There have been instances where the Researcher got so carried away in the reading, that on cross examination later was unable to recall anything about the state of the genitals. Take heed.

3. Grab a hold of that shaft and give it a vigorous stroking—get it good and hard. If you have any trouble with this step, consult a sex book or talk to a knowledgable friend. Notice if he is pointing right or left. Is it the same way he hangs? This could be very significant. Has the head flared out or remained in the same proportion to the shaft? Or has it actually proportionally gotten smaller? Has the overall size of the penis become tremendously enlarged, or is it just standing upright at about the same size? Has the penis taken on a distinctly different shape or character, putting it into another class? You will be using all this data in your evaluation.

4. Finally get him to stand again and see if the penis points up, out, or down. Get out the ruler and protractor and measure the lenght of that hard rod, and the angle at which it is pointing.

This is basically all the information you will need to work up a full reading after the session.

The Female

1. The first action is to move in slowly on her bush. Note its color and density.

2. Next you'll have to get her legs well spread and, using your fingers, open up her labia—gently if you please. You can get fooled if you don't get the labia well exposed. Try not to get her too excited at first as this will cause the labia to swell and throw off the reading. There will be plenty of time for that later.

3. Begin the examination. Is the majora large and crowding the minora, or does the minora stand out proudly from the folds of

the majora? If she is the Slit type the minora will be almost completely hidden in the majora. Write down the size relationships between the labia, and whether the minora is hidden or standing out.

4. Next notice if there are any unusual markings or freckles. Where are they located? Note the color. Are those luscious lips a light pink or do they lean toward rosy red?

5. Now examine the clitoris. This little jewel is a fund of information, so take care. Is it exposed and standing out for all to see, or is it hidden shyly in its hood? Is it large or small? Finally wet your finger (or use your tongue) and get the clit erect. What degree of enlargement did it attain? If it was hidden did it become exposed? These are the vital points you will need to do a complete reading. Get it all down in your notebook.

You now have all the information you need to do the evaluation. At this point you may want to take a short break from the reading to take care of the subject at hand. Where you take it from here is up to you. Enjoy!

Reading Form
Male

1. Pants off ☐
2. Shower (Optional but recommended) ☐
3. **Hang**
   a) Direction: Left ☐   Right ☐   Straight ☐
   b) Length:
   c) Angle of Dangle:
   d) Tip: Up ☐   Down ☐   Straight ☐
4. **Head**
   a) Large ☐   Small ☐
   b) Flat ☐   Pointed ☐   Flared ☐
5. **Shaft**
   a) Long ☐   Short ☐
   b) Thick ☐   Thin ☐
   c) Bent? ☐   Degree of Bend:
6. **Unusual Markings and Interesting Oddities**
   a) Freckles ☐   Where
   b) Moles ☐   Where
   c) Tattoos ☐   Where
   d) Others ☐   Where
   e) None of the above ☐
7. **Erect The Penis**
   a) Head: Flared Out ☐   Remained the same ☐
   b) Proportion of head to shaft:
      Larger ☐
      Smaller ☐
      Same ☐
   d) Degree of enlargement upon erection:
      Normal enlargement ☐
      Great enlargement ☐
      Awesome enlargement ☐
   e) Character/Shape change ☐
8. **Direction of Erection**
   a) Left ☐   Right ☐   Straight ☐
   b) Upward ☐   Forward ☐   Downward ☐
   c) Angle of Point:
9) **Notes:**

Reading Form
Female

1. Panties off ☐
2. Shower (Optional but recommended) ☐
3. **Bush**
   a) Color: Light ☐   Dark ☐
   b) Density: Thick ☐   Thin ☐   Wispy ☐
4. **Labia**
   a) Majora: Large ☐   Small ☐
   b) Minora: Large ☐   Small ☐
   c) Color: Rosy Red ☐   Pink ☐
5. **Unusual markings and interesting oddities**
   a) Freckles ☐   Where
   b) Moles ☐   Where
   c) Tattoos ☐   Where
   d) Unique Folds ☐   Where
   e) Other ☐   Where
   f) None of the above ☐
6. **Clitoris**
   a) Hidden ☐   Exposed ☐
   b) Large ☐   Small ☐
   c) Degree of Enlargement
      Normal Enlargement ☐
      Great Enlargement ☐
      Astonishing Enlargement ☐
7. **Notes:**

Matched
Pairs

Matched Pairs

In a basic sense this is the most important section in the book. Let's face it, we all want to know what the people we are dealing with are like. And when it comes to sex we want to know how we are going to match up with the people we meet. In this section we have had to "rewrite the book".

The last major Genitological study to address the area of genital compatibility was the Kama Sutra, almost 2500 years ago. It is obvious that the world has come a long way since then. An understanding of modern times coupled with a full understanding of Genitology was necessary to produce a truly modern analysis of the compatibility question.

The following appraisals are of necessity short. This is still a burgeoning young field, and only the outlines have been drawn. Research will continue—perhaps you yourself will contribute to the growing understanding as you expose your relationships to the golden light of Genitological wisdom!

Code

Male		Female	
0000	Dynamite	♠♠♠♠	Dynamite
000	Fireworks	♠♠♠	Fireworks
00	Sparks	♠♠	Sparks
0	A Dud	♠	A Dud
O	Forget it!	O	Forget it!

Erection
Connections

The Nightstick / The Cock

Lady Finger / The Pearl ❶❶❶
Here is a babe the Nightstick wants to score with. But when he does, that's it, he throws the Pearl back in to the sea.

Big Mama / The Mouth ❶❶❶❶
This can be a very robust two fisted love affair for the Cock. The Big Mama at her best can stand up to all the Cock can thrust at her, and give it right back. He can't toss her off.

Prissy Pussy / The Rosebud ❶
The Nightstick would enjoy deflowering the Rosebud, just to put a little pizzaz in her puss. But of course he would leave her petalless.

Venus Man Trap / The Butterfly ❶❶❶❶
Here his wildness matches her wiles. She can keep him interested as she flits just out of his grasp, and somehow, even though he gets her in the end, he can never quite have her. It keeps him coming back.

The Slit / The Split Tail ❶❶❶❶
His golden bannana will razzle-dazzle the Slit. She is attracted to this strong masculine man.

The Stogey / The Spike

Lady Finger / The Pearl ❶❶❶
They are really from two different worlds, but if he gets the Pearl he's gotten a real treasure. If he's the political type she'll smooth out his social life, and may get him elected.

Big Mama / The Mouth ❶❶❶❶
He'd love her to toke on his stogey any day. They are a rollicking pair and they make mean hot spicy love together.

108

Prissy Pussy / The Rosebud 🍩🍩

He'd love to unprissy her pussy and hang the beaver pelt on the wall.

Venus Man Trap / The Butterfly 🍩🍩🍩

The Spike likes her street toughness. He'd like to pin her down, but look out she may trap him first.

The Slit / The Split Tail 🍩🍩🍩

The Stogey burns with desire for the Slit. Plucking this innocent peach really appeals to his manliness.

The Dented Dick / The Crank

Lady Finger / The Pearl 🍩🍩

The Crank would like to play on her hidden desires. But if he is going to succeed in tickling the Lady Finger's fantasies he'll have to come on with a bit of savoir-faire.

Big Mama / The Mouth 🍩🍩🍩

The Dented Dick appreciates the Big Mama because she enjoys his novelties. This guy can really crank her up.

Prissy Pussy / The Rosebud 🍩

The Crank finds the Prissy Pussy a great challange. His major attraction is to despoil her neat rose garden and move on.

Venus Man Trap / The Butterfly 🍩🍩🍩🍩

These two are really the kooks of kink. Their typical reaction when they meet is "At last! Somebody I can play out my wildest wet dreams with."

The Slit / The Split Tail 🍩🍩🍩🍩

Naturally the Slit appeals to the glorious eroticism of the Crank. He'd just love to run his fantasies in, out, around and through the Slit.

Le Long Carabine / The Shaft

Lady Finger / The Pearl ◗◗◗
The Shaft likes her intellegence. She can keep up with his game of verbal wit, and that will keep him interested longer than most. But eventually he'll leave her with an empty shell, having plucked her Pearl.

Big Mama / The Mouth ◗
The Mama is much too down to earth to fall for his line of bullshit. Of all the woman she seems to see through his masquerade better than any.

Prissy Pussy / The Rosebud ◗◗
The Carabine likes the game of seducing the timid Rosebud. This is a job requiring the utmost skill, and he enjoys weaving his web to ensnare her. Of course after the seduction he leaves her like all the rest.

Venus Man Trap / The Butterfly ◗◗◗◗
Here is the woman who can match his tricks. They both know the game so well that there is no question of anybody being fooled. They respect each other as worthy opponents, and often end up friends.

The Slit / The Split Tail ◗◗◗◗
This one drives him wild. Just the idea of spreading those young thighs will keep him working on her for months.

The Pinky / The Bamboo Shoot

Lady Finger / The Pearl ◗◗◗
For the Pinky, the Pearl could add the lustre he needs to succeed in his social life. This would be a good catch for the him.

Big Mama / The Mouth ◗
The Pinky could float in her expansiveness, but more likely he'll drown.

Prissy Pussy / The Rosebud 0000
Pinky, this Bud's for you!

Venus Man Trap / The Butterfly 0
Pinkys may be attracted to this one. But watch out little Pinky, the Venus Man Trap could eat your bamboo shoot alive.

The Slit / The Split Tail 0000
Strangly this is the one type of woman who can arouse a spark of sexual interest in the Pinky. His likelihood of getting and then holding her are almost nil. But watch carefully, that wimpy professor will get a bit of letch in his eye as he looks her over.

The Princely Pistol / The Wand

Lady Finger / The Pearl 0000
This lady can really twirl the Pistol. This is quite a match. With her hot little finger on his trigger there will be nothing but rapid fire bulls eyes.

Big Mama / The Mouth 0 0
If he can get by her mouth he's got it made. Her bedroom antics will more than make up for the effort. This is usually a one shot affair.

Prissy Pussy / The Rosebud 0
She may satisfy him with some intellectual magic, but she won't satisfy his magic wand.

Venus Man Trap / The Butterfly 0
This Butterfly may look like a sweet treat, but it's only bait for the trap. Let your wand wander elsewhere.

The Slit / The Split Tail 0 0 0
His immediate attraction for her sweet innocence will drive him wild. But this is usually short lived. He needs the thrust of a deeper relationship.

The Dork / The Pud

Lady Finger / The Pearl 0000
For the successful Dork the Pearl would supply the social wit and charm that he definitely lacks. But only as a successful hard driving businessman could he possess the Pearl. It is her fascination with power that would seduce her.

Big Mama / The Mouth 00
This pair is a lesson in coarseness and it is often very funny. She can match him joke for joke and drink for drink. But if they end up battling for control it will be a battle royale.

Prissy Pussy / The Rosebud 0
This pussy is to prissy for the hearty Dork.

Venus Man Trap / The Butterfly 000
The elusive Butterfly might just let herself get caught in the Dork's web of money. She will mesmerize him with her flutterings.

The Slit / The Split Tail 0000
Her love and need for strong men will attract the Slit to the Dork. He loves to ravish these tasty morsels.

The Toad Stool / The Putz

Lady Finger / The Pearl 00
To capture her would be a gem of a lifetime, but to keep her would be impossible.

Big Mama / The Mouth 0
Don't tangle with this one little Toad Stool. She'll whang dangle your doodle like you've never seen before.

Prissy Pussy / The Rosebud 0000
This couple makes a great pair watching late night TV and eating crackers in bed. Their once a month passion is perfect.

112

Venus Man Trap / The Butterfly 0
The Putz might get caught in the magic of butterfly wings, but the Venus Man Trap will only chop and saute his Toad Stool.

The Slit / The Split Tail 000
If he can catch her, her school girl antics will get his putz-a-pumpin'. You can go full blast here.

Pussy Pleasers

The Venus Man Trap / The Butterfly

Nightstick / The Cock ♦♦♦♦
This is a 4-Star steel belted radial love affaire.

Le Long Carabine / The Shaft ♦♦♦
These two can really tango or really tangle. They will both fight for the upper hand in the relationship. This one will produce star-spangled fireworks or dynamite.

Dork / The Pud ♦
This is purely a business deal. She'd put up with him for his money. She likes to live high and he can supply.

Dented Dick / The Crank ♦♦♦
There is a bit of perversity in both of their natures. This is a chemistry of kink.

Princely Pistol / The Wand ♦♦♦
Very often this begins with a magnetic attraction and ends with an atomic explosion.

Stogey / The Spike ♦♦
These two understand each other. They are both street wise and tough. This is a hard hitting passionate adventure.

Toad Stool / The Putz 0
For the Butterfly to get involved with this type would be purely a calculated maneuver in one of her schemes.

Pinky / The Bamboo Shoot ♦
She will eat this boy alive. Her steel trap will snap down on his tender shoot.

The Slit / The Split Tail

Nightstick / The Cock ♦♦♦♦
The Cock epitomizes the desires of the Slit. Strong and domineering he will hypnotize the young Slit. Fortunately he has a soft spot for her sweet innocence.

116

Le Long Carabine / The Shaft ♪♪♪
This sophisticated knowledgeable guy will impress the naive Slit.
Whether she can keep him interested is another matter.

Dork / The Pud ♪♪♪
This bohunk can satisfy her deepest craving for protection. This
Pud's for you.

Dented Dick / The Crank ♪
If the Slit is interested in exploring the world of exotic delights
this is the man for her. Otherwise she had better steer clear.

Princely Pistol / The Wand ♪♪
The Slit will be enchanted by the Wand. But he is only a flash of
magic, she needs more manliness than he's willing to muster.

Stogey / The Spike ♪♪♪♪
The Slit will be attracted to the strong rumba beat of the macho
Spike. His very male vibration will send her split tail quivering.

Toad Stool / The Putz ♪
She'll have to watch out for the lecherous Putz. That seemingly
nerdy professor could be trying to get his cold clammy hands on
her bazoombas.

Pinky / The Bamboo Shoot ♪
Let's face it, the Pinky is not the Slit's manly male. He couldn't
protect his cookies from a cockroach.

The Prissy Pussy / The Rosebud

Nightstick / The Cock ♪
No way, Jose. The Nightstick would pull the Rosebud up by the
roots and crush the petals in his fist.

Le Long Carabine / The Shaft ♪
The Rosebud has to watch out for this one. She may be attracted.
But she's sure to get shafted.

Dork / The Pud ♠

If the Prissy Pussy is looking for a business partner the Pud could be a 4-star match. But sexually the Pud would wilt the Bud.

Dented Dick / The Crank ♠

The Prissy Pussy would find this relationship about as appealing as a date with King Kong. The foibles of the Dented Dick would drive her crazy.

Princely Pistol / The Wand ♠ ♠ ♠

They have a common love of poetry but his love ends at the bookshelf. She simply doesn't have the spark to ignite the Wand.

Stogey / The Spike ♠ ♠

This is an attraction of opposites. If this one makes it, it's because he is the bully male and she is the doting female. Sexually there could be fireworks. He pounding on the bathroom door demanding sex, she hiding shyly in the tub.

Toad Stool / The Putz ♠ ♠ ♠

These are similar souls but they may clash because they're so close in character. If anybody can get the Toad Stool up it is the Rosebud, and the Toad Stool is the only known type to have ever gotten the Prissy Pussy's panties measurably wet.

Pinky / The Bamboo Shoot ♠ ♠ ♠ ♠

The Pinky and the Prissy Pussy are perfectly matched. Though much of the time they will be discussing Milton and Chaucer, when they do tango it will be more like a waltz.

The Big Mama / The Mouth

Nightstick / The Cock ♠ ♠ ♠

These two can really rock and roll. She can match his brashness line for line. If they get competitive, then the fur really flies. Naturally they're great in bed.

Le Long Carabine / The Shaft ♦♦

She's too down to earth to get sucked in by his smooth line. She'll probably tell him to cut the crap and buzz off. If they ever do make it to the bedroom its fantastic (* * * *) ! His long shaft is a real match for her snatch.

Dork / The Pud ♦♦♦♦

If you find the Big Mama sitting around bars with her butt hanging over the stool, you'll likely find the Dork beside her. And as a pair in the office they can't be beat. They love to sit around for hours telling each other dirty jokes.

Dented Dick / The Crank ♦♦♦♦

The Big Mama has no inhibitions, she'll try anything, as long as it is exciting. She can't wait to get her hands on his randy root. She loves to find someone as wild as she is.

Princely Pistol / The Wand ♦♦

The wand is a bit too mushy for her, but she does like the way he twirls his Pistol.

Stogey / The Spike ♦♦♦

They can both dish it out and take it. You might think they are fighting, but as far as they are concerned its just love coos.

Toad Stool / The Putz 0

If this relationship gets started at all, it will not last long. Nerds are not her forte.

Pinky / The Bamboo Shoot ♦

Observers have reported overhearing comments like "Is it up ?" "Am I supposed to use a microscope?", and "Where is it?" coming through bedroom walls.

The Lady Finger / The Pearl

Nightstick / The Cock ♦♦♦

This could be good for a fast fling. The Nightstick and the Lady Finger being traditional opposites may find delight for one night.

Le Long Carabine / The Shaft ♦♦♦
Le Long Carabine may snatch the Pearl only to leave her with an empty shell in the end. She can be easily taken by his sophisticated roguishness.

Dork / The Pud ♦
The Dork's insensitivity will dull the Pearl. Though there may be interest on the business level. The Pearl will only show her jewels to him in a conference room.

Dented Dick / The Crank ♦
The Dented Dick is not likely to dent the Pearl. But she may find a momentary interest in his oddity thus satisfying that sometimes roving Lady Finger.

Princely Pistol / The Wand ♦♦♦♦
Put the Princely Pistol and the Lady Finger together and she will soon have her finger on his trigger. This romance is not just a shot in the dark, it is meant to last.

Stogey / The Spike ♦♦
The Spike would be an instant sexual adventure for the Pearl. We might say a bit of a 'spike of life' but just a dash, because she would lose interest fast.

Toad Stool / The Putz 0
The Toad Stool is invisible to the Pearl, a nonentity. She does not know he even exists.

Pinky / The Bamboo Shoot ♦♦
Sexually it will be milk toast. Socially it could be the talk of the campus.

Climax

By now you should have a good overview of the principles of Genitology. But mind you it is only an overview. The purpose of this book has been to show the possibilities, and hopefully to stimulate the population to swell the ranks of Genitologists with new blood. Even though it is an ancient science, it is by no means fully explored. We now issue a call to the people of the world to rise up and embrace this new science as their own. The potential for new discoveries fairly abounds.

We are always open to the influx of new research data. Much of the material in this book is the result of observations made by field researchers. We have tried to indicate areas requiring further study. But as in any burgeoning young science one cannot hope to fully grasp the growth of a concept while others are adding their creative input to the process. Probably in the last analysis what we want to say here is go forth, seek out, and investigate. Please let us know what you find. And above all—ENJOY!

Glossary

Glossary

Bazoombas: Pural for bosom. Usually gigantic

Bearded Clam: A hippy vagina

Beaver: A small animal that chews on stiff poles

Bush: A green leafy plant usually used ornamentally

Clit: The soft spot in every women's heart

Cock: The long honkin' dong

Dick: Jane's and Spot's best friend

Dong: A dinger (also known as a donger) in a bell

Donkey Dong: A porno video game

Genitology: The study of the genitals

Golden Banana: A bar in the San Fernando Valley, as in, "Lets go for a drink at The Golden Banana"

Hole or the Black Hole: A place where male virginity mysteriously disappears and is never seen again

Horny: To want to blow your own or someone else's horn. Be it a trumpet, sousaphone, trombone or bullhorn

Hot Box: A wienie warmer

Hot Rod: A dynamite dong

How's It Hanging: A greeting

Jade Gates: The tender trap

Jewels, The Family: The treasure found between the legs of men

Jewelry Box: The receptacle found between the legs of women

Long Honkin' Dong: An express train that runs between New York City and Washington D.C.

Macho Meat: The twat—a delectable hors d'oeuvre

Muff Diver: A skin diver with ear muffs

Pecker: A red headed double breasted pussy whomper indigenous to the single swingers' swamp

Pee Pee: Short for Pygmy Penis

Peter: A name for a dong. Derived from the Bible

Pounding The Pud: Choking the chicken

Prick: A nickname for Peter

Pussy: A warm furry friendly pet

Pussy Whipped: To be flogged by an enraged twat

Ram Rod: A big horn sheep's whanger

Root: The basis of life from which all nourishment spurts

Snatch: To steal a piece of ass

Thick Stick: The third leg

Tight Pussy: An intoxicated cat

Twat: A word to begin a question, as in, "Twat, I cunt hear you, bare-ass me again"

Whack His Pee Pee: Orginated as a punishment for an adulterer during the Inquisition

Whang Dangle Your Doodle: What you do all night long

Whanger: Derived from the word twang, a sound made by a very stiff dick when plucked, as in, "Twang your magic whanger, Froggy"

YOU WILL ALSO WANT TO READ:

☐ **85120 Twisted Image,** *by Ace Backwords.* This is the first collection of comic strips by America's funniest underground cartoonist. Ace Backwords takes on the controversial topics of sex, drugs and modern culture. His strips have appeared in more than 200 "marginal" publications including *High Times, Maximum Rock'n'Roll, Screw* and the Loompanics Catalog. *For Adults Only. 1990, 8½ x 11, 128 pp, more than 200 strips, soft cover.* **$12.95.**

☐ **64129 Sell Yourself To Science, The Complete Guide to Selling Your Organs, Body Fluids, Bodily Functions and Being A Human Guinea Pig,** *by Jim Hogshire.* This book shows exactly what your body is worth and how to sell it, in whole or in part. Your body is your business when you sell renewable resources such as blood, sperm, milk and hair. You can also arrange to sell your heart, lungs and other vital organs in the most unusual "going out of business" sale you've ever heard of. This amazing "career guide" also reveals what it's like to work as a guinea pig for drug companies. It pays up to $100 a day and this book lists more than 150 active test sites. *1992, 5½ x 8½, 168 pp, illustrated, soft cover.* **$16.95.**

☐ **85102 Recreational Drugs,** *by Professor Buzz.* The single finest book ever written on the manufacture of recreational drugs. Profusely illustrated, it covers equipment, techniques and reagents used in the clandestine manufacture of illegal drugs. Procedures for crystallization, chromatography, distillation and reductions are give for amphetamines, hallucinogens, THC, analgesics, hypnotics, sedatives and tranquilizers. Also includes detailed instructions for buying and making precursors. *Sold for informational purposes only. 1989, 8½ x 11, 166 pp, illustrated, soft cover.* **$21.95.**

▼▼GEN94

LOOMPANICS UNLIMITED
PO BOX 1197
PORT TOWNSEND, WA 98368
206-385-2230

Please send me the titles I have checked above. I have enclosed $_____ which includes $4.00 for the shipping and handling of 1 to 3 books, $6.00 for 4 or more. (Washington residents please include 7.9% sales tax.)

Name_____

Address _____

City _____

State/Zip _____

Now accepting Visa and MasterCard.